Contents

What to Do 2

The Home of Whales 4

Orcas Away from their Home 6

Wild Animals 8

A Different World 10

Setting an Orca Free 12

Keiko – A Film Star 14

Something to Think About 16

Do You Need to Find an Answer? 18

Do You Want to Find Out More? 19

Word Help 20

Location Help 23

Index 24

What to Do

Choose a face

Remember the colour you have chosen.

When you see your face on the page, you are the LEADER.

The LEADER reads the text in the speech bubbles.

There are extra words and questions to help you on the teacher's whiteboard. The LEADER reads these aloud.

When you see this stop sign, the LEADER reads it aloud.

STOP
My predictions were right/wrong because . . .

You might need:

- to look at the WORD HELP on pages 20–22;
- to look at the LOCATION HELP on page 23;
- an atlas.

If you are the **LEADER**, follow these steps:

1 PREDICT

Think about what is on the page.

- Say to your group:

"I am looking at this page and I think it is going to be about . . ."

- Tell your group:

"Read the page to yourselves."

2 CLARIFY

Talk about words and their meaning.

- Say to your group:

"Are there any words you don't know?"

"Is there anything else on the page you didn't understand?"

- Talk about the words and their meanings with your group.
- Read the whiteboard.

Let's check:

- Ask your group to find the LET'S CHECK word in the WORD HELP on pages 20–22. Ask them to read the meaning of the word aloud.

3 ASK QUESTIONS

Talk about how to find out more.

- Say to your group:

"Who has a question about what we have read?"

- Question starters are: how..., why..., when..., where..., what..., who...
- Read the question on the whiteboard and talk about it with your group.

4 SUMMARISE

Think about who and what the story was mainly about.

This page was mainly about fact fact

When you get to pages 16–17, you can talk to a partner or write and draw on your own.

or

The Home of Whales

Orca whales live in the sea. This is their home. In the sea, they can swim where they want to. There are no fences to keep them in one place. The orcas are **free**.

In the sea, orcas don't **attack** people. When orcas are taken away from their home, it can be different.

I am looking at this page and I think it is going to be about... because...

Are there any words you don't know?

Let's check: attack

Who has a question about what we have read?

What might be different about an animal that is away from its home?

An orca is sometimes called a killer whale.

This page was mainly about ... fact fact

STOP
My predictions were right/wrong because . . .

Orcas Away from their Home

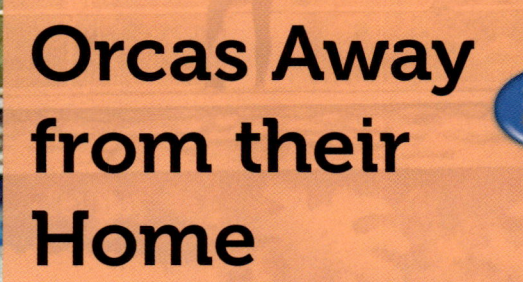

People have caught orcas and put them in pools. They have **trained** them to do **tricks**. Sometimes the tricks have gone wrong. Orcas have attacked their **trainers**. Some trainers have died.

Now, some people say orcas should not be taken away from their home in the sea.

I am looking at this page and I think it is going to be about… because…

Are there any words you don't know?

Who has a question about what we have read?

Let's check: trained

Why do you think orcas might attack their trainers?

A trainer teaches an orca to do tricks.

This page was mainly about

fact
fact

STOP
My predictions were right/wrong because . . .

Wild Animals

I am looking at this page and I think it is going to be about… because…

Orcas are **wild animals**. In the sea they live with other orcas. They can live a long time. However, they don't live as long when they are taken away from their home.

The first orca that was caught only lived for a day. It just swam round and round the pool. It kept **banging** into the sides.

Are there any words you don't know?

Let's check: wild animals

Who has a question about what we have read?

Why do you think the orca swam round and round the pool?

This is a family of orcas in their sea home.

This page was mainly about... fact fact

STOP
My predictions were right/wrong because . . .

A Different World

I am looking at this page and I think it is going to be about… because…

Some people think that orcas change when they are not in their home. A trainer cannot always know what an orca might do.

In the sea, an orca can swim a long way in a day. It can't swim far in a pool.

In a pool, some orcas live **alone**. It is a very different place from their home.

Are there any words you don't know?

Who has a question about what we have read?

Let's check: alone

Why do you think a trainer cannot always know what an orca might do?

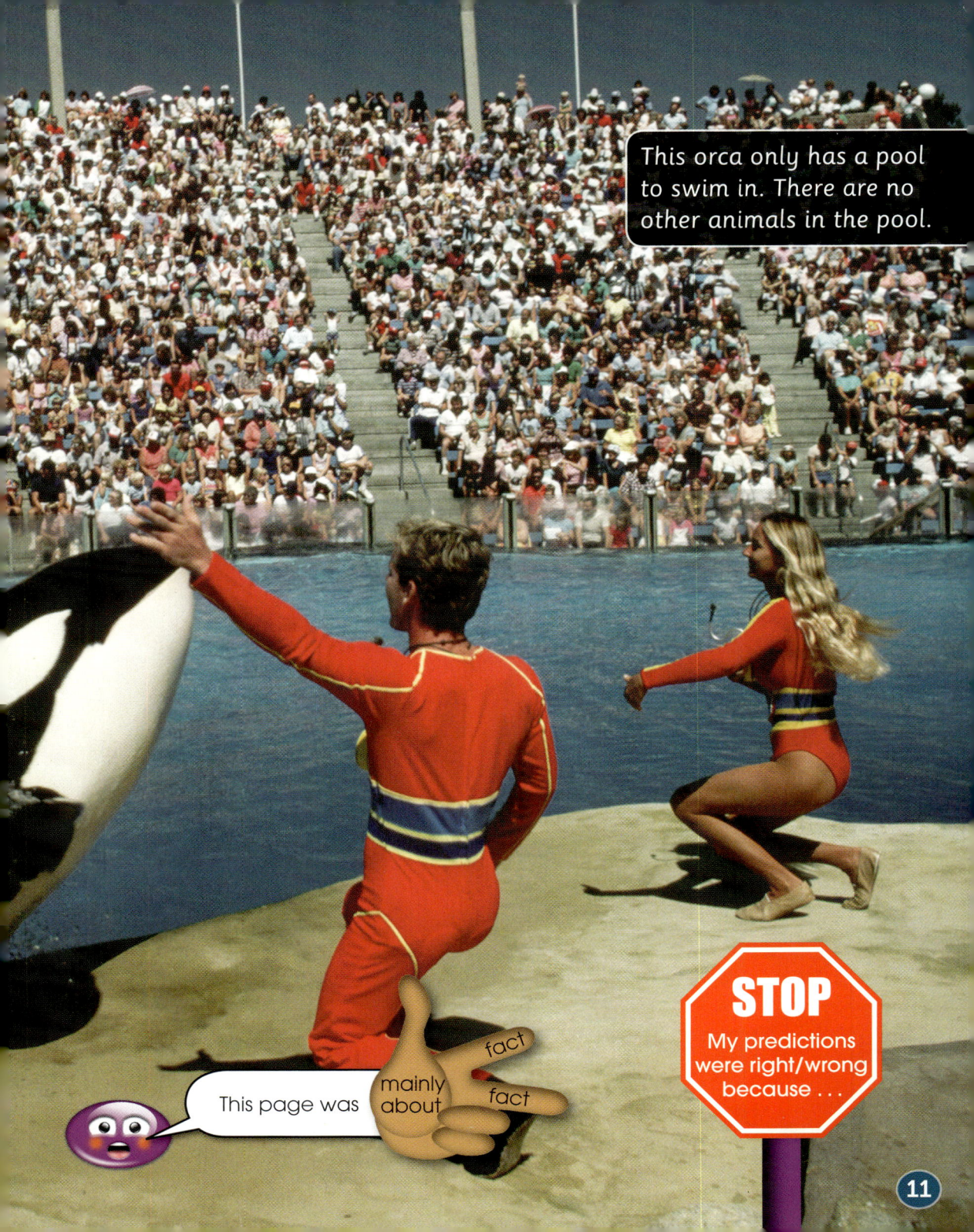

This orca only has a pool to swim in. There are no other animals in the pool.

This page was mainly about... fact fact

STOP My predictions were right/wrong because...

Setting an Orca Free

I am looking at this page and I think it is going to be about... because...

Many people think that orcas should be set free. However, an orca can't just be put back in the sea. First, a **pen** is made in the sea. The orca has to stay in this for a while.

When the orca is set free, it may not be able to find a family **pod**.

Are there any words you don't know?

Who has a question about what we have read?

Let's check:
pod

Why do you think an orca has to stay in a pen for a while?

Trainers are moving the orca to the sea pen.

an orca sea pen

This page was mainly about... fact fact

STOP
My predictions were right/wrong because...

Keiko – A Film Star

Keiko was an orca. He was a **film star**. He was put back in the sea after 23 years.

Keiko never found a family pod. So, he was looked after by people again. When he was 27 years old, he got very ill and died.

Keiko couldn't live by himself in the sea. He had forgotten how to be free.

I am looking at this page and I think it is going to be about… because…

Are there any words you don't know?

Let's check:
journey

Who has a question about what we have read?

Do you think Keiko should have been a film star? Why?

Iceland

Norway

Keiko made this long **journey** alone after he was set free, but he did not look after himself.

This page was mainly about

fact

fact

STOP
My predictions were right/wrong because . . .

Something to Think About

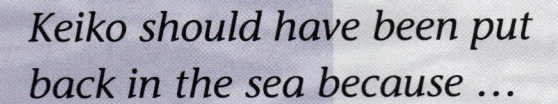

Keiko should have been put back in the sea because …

Think about the story of Keiko. Read the words below then talk about your ideas with a partner, or write them down.

Keiko should not have been put back in the sea because ...

Do You Need to Find an Answer?

You could go to . . .

Library >

Expert >

Internet >

Do You Want to Find Out More?

You could look in books or on the internet. These key words could help you:

animals doing tricks

animals in pods

animal trainers

film star animals

Keiko

killer whale

orca

Word Help

Dictionary

alone	not with others
attack	to try and harm someone by fighting
banging	hitting something hard
film star	a famous person or animal who is in a film
free	nothing to stop you from doing something or from going somewhere
journey	a trip from one place to another
pen	an area with a fence around it to keep animals in

pod	a family group or a group of the same sea mammals
trained	taught a person or an animal how to do something
trainers	people who train other people or animals
tricks	actions like jumping through a ring or balancing a ball
wild animals	animals that live in the wild where they are not looked after by people

Word Help

Thesaurus

attack	hit, hurt, harm
banging	hitting, beating, knocking
pen	cage

Location Help

Where do Orcas Live?

Where orcas are found.

Where orcas won't be found.

Index

Keiko 14–15

pen 12–13

people 4, 6, 10, 12, 14–15

pod 12, 14

pool 6, 8, 10–11

sea 4, 8–9, 10, 12–13, 14

trainer 6–7, 10, 13

tricks 6–7

wild 8